ODDBITS**OF**BROKEN**THINGS**

poems by todd regoulinsky

BIG BLACK CAT PRESS
Old Orchard Beach, Maine

Copyright 2008 by Todd Regoulinsky
ISBN: 978-0-6152-2271-4

All rights reserved. No part of this book may be reprinted or reproduced in any form without permission unless for the purpose of review or citation.

Cover photo and inside portrait taken by Todd Regoulinsky. Cover design and layout by Todd Regoulinsky and 276 Design.

First edition, printed in the United States of America.

For more information, please visit:
www.toddregoulinsky.com
www.oddbitsofbrokenthings.com

contents

all you can ask for	1
why i don't do poetry readings	2
God, Part 3	5
7 and one quarter inches	7
advice	8
Room 311	9
junkie	11
reel	12
rimshot	13
legal graffiti	14
11.18.98	16
falling on the grenade	17
an open letter to Charles Simic	19
therapy	21
suicide every morning	22
wise man of the traffic jam	24
turbulence	28
suck honey from fuchsia	29
voices on the platform	31
solitaire	32
sucker punch	34
peace in our time	36
sea wall	38
a love letter to Mrs. Castro	40
sometimes, a wonder of wild roses	41
delight in your eyes	43
no long goodbyes	44

August rains	46
greetings from wherever you are:	48
the sweet science	49
i never wear a watch	51
temperamental animals	52
miller time	54
one minute short of forever	57
the luckiest man alive	59
choices	61
get in the car	63
gurrrlllz	66
the world dies each sunday at 7:38 pm	68
Ben Carr at the Alamo	70
the job description	72
Mr. Ani DiFranco	74
collect	76
all the sweet women are gone	78
high noon	79
idiot savant	80
lifespan	82
resting in the hours and minutes	83
black and white newsreel	85
the ultimate reward	88
because someone should;	90
Love, in the Nuclear Age	91
Todo se aparta sin danar la hora	93
You're sleeping in the next room	95
to my little cherry bomb -	97
all of them there in a row	98

for Kim and Kaelin

all you can ask for:

is to find a parking space downtown
        among the buildings and zombies
not to get mugged at the grocery store
a good cup of coffee
avoid being minced in the crosswalk
        by the suicide machines
make a warm home of each moment
find enough change for a 6 pack in the couch
unwind the song of raindrop bombardiers
one or two good ideas
to occasionally pull a joker instead
        of the ace of hearts
three or ten solid words
dodge the bullet of infatuation
        and fall in love
        with a beautiful, honest woman
        as full of perfections and defects
        as yourself.
failing all this,
        if it's midnight laying in your bed,
        cool breeze from the window
        under roof
        not starving (too much)
        and still breathing...

it's been a good day.

why i don't do poetry readings

so this poet walks into the room, black-clad
through the shadows:
a nervous nicotine twitch, dark circles under eyes,
weight of the collected works of Ezra Pound on his shoulders –
and he begins reading into the microphone,
not looking up
and he's doing okay, ya know?

he's been dying to read this outloud since the words came
unwelcomed and unwanted
in the middle of the night,
since he'd felt that 10-penny nail through his soul
twisting him around.
excitement comes from the depths at the words finally
sent into the world after wondering if this could be it.

his red wheelbarrow – his road diverging in the wood.
white knuckled fist around the mike stand, a crutch holding
his mind up around the body after no sleep for three days,
writing and rewriting the same stanzas, puzzling the words
into place,
and it's just so, just so oh-so-perfect now...

somewhere in the audience a rustle of papers, a clink of glasses,
the spell is beginning to break and the man with a face like

repentance in the third row left to use the pisser.
he notices their impatience – how they want it now, want it
better, want it all: neat and clean and with a punchline and
frustrated poet-esque with just a subtle twist of words on the
side. the poet begins to fidget himself into a corner, dragging
the microphone along with him – retreating
but refusing to surrender to the moment.

everybody's a critic. everybody's a martyr. everyone is waiting.

now the thoughts run together into a nightmare reel: this is his
Waterloo, his *Ishtar,* his event horizon...
the moment from which no recovery is possible –
terminal velocity of the
literary kamikaze dive.

there she is though. sitting pristine as cherry blossoms
before the breeze
in the second row.
she nods and smiles with the words despite his hesitance,
despite his fear, despite the crippled twist he's put
into his spine.
now he fights his way back out of the corner, cutting the air
again and searing wounds closed with a firebrand. he rallies
like a boxer with nothing
left to lose.

everybody's a critic. everybody's a martyr. everyone is waiting.

... then from the fourth row, somewhere on the right,
this guy lobs a perfectly over-ripened tomato
(God only knows where he got it at this time of night)
and the poet watches it land at his feet. splat.

everybody's a critic. everybody's a martyr. everyone is waiting.

now the girl in the second row is pissed, and she turns around
to level the audience with her gaze. before anything comes
before everything, it happens.

three shots ring out through the smoke-filled spotlight
and the sweating twitching nervous poet falls back
out of the spotlight,
microphone still clutched in hand, into a shadowy heap.

from the rear comes the cry of "Sic semper poetus!"
and the stranger runs out the side door at top speed,
nearly toppling the cappuccino machine.

everybody's a critic. everybody's a martyr. everyone is waiting.

God, Part 3

God is a poet – roaming and stalking
sidewalks of the world:
an empty trenchcoat that is 125 shades of gray
gray of twilight morning
pockmarked concrete slab gray.
like William Burroughs strung out on junk –
gaunt with skin alternately draped
and stretched over hollow bones –
pages falling out of coat pockets
scattering in the street
dripping words oozing off the fiber
like liquid cancer onto cobblestone.
Sigh and wheeze   gimp and limp
Left and right   until pain is routine.
fading like soggy newsprint,
he mutters of his 7 days of fame:
"too quick and all wrong...."
edging forward along the cracks
where poets embrace entropy,
old gods go to die –
and it is tombstone quiet.
our father who art in poetry
hallowed be thy pen:
dried out and weary, ashes to ether
over puddles....

over garbage cans....

over skyscrapers....

over grayness into clouds.

7 and one quarter inches

of space between
2 objects at 3 AM.

life is a word problem –
(our lips not meeting
always moving halfway
never to touch)
with no quick answers, only
question marks and
the occasional
exclamation point.

i do not show my work
holding fear and insecurity close
not sure what will happen when our lips touch –
afraid that the world might vanish from under us
leaving two objects at 3 AM
clinging to each other in nothingness

staring into eyes I've seen but never knew
before a few moments ago,
this whole world could crash in
on these 7 and one quarter inches
and i'd never know it.

advice

kiss these only :

wind

eternity

love after rain

sweet wild nectar.

but not this methodical morning where

shy ominous whispers grope

the cool hell of concrete in the machine.

fragrant liquor of your love   a dream

of flawless romance

is a delirious shadow across us.

Room 311

it's May when i go to the store
sometime after 8 pm
and retrieve cold Irish beer
from the large chrome lit boxes in back
along with a package of Phillies Blunts.
climb the staircase to the third floor,
down the hall past loud music
and whispering voices -
she's waiting for me to arrive, window
open to the cool night breeze.
about to take a chair,
"dance with me" she says,
turning the music louder and
crossing the simple room in
three light steps.
and we did –
thighs touching mine
hot breath and giggles on my neck.
venturing out with bottles in tow,
we laughed and kissed the night air
blowing smoke-rings over town.
we drunkstumbled through strange backyards
laughed over the fences
dodging unknown watchdogs in the moonlight.
we raised the sun on our shoulders

calling each other by secret names,

thinking this moment couldn't pass

as it did into another....

when I left she was nearly asleep

on clean white angelic sheets

a soft blonde curl laid masterfully

across her face

for all the world

to see.

junkie

my hands are trembling from too many cups of coffee.
(two teaspoons of you stirred in)
searching for you, searching for a fix, searching for
a cure to what ails me
my blood hungers for you
a drug
more potent than the horse 'Trane flooded
himself with before discovering a love supreme
more addictive than oxygen
    (but twice as sweet
    as the smile on your
    lips, twice as sweet
    as the starlight in
    your hair)
my heart beats empty without my
sugary elixir.
I'm an addict, I admit – so put me in a meeting
and this one will proudly stand with
nametag over my heart
Styrofoam cup in my shaking grip
professing my yen
admitting my weakness
and display the track marks you left –
my only and sweetest memory.

reel

we drive and play poetry

only always all summer

in bed I heave beneath pedestrian

skin   frantic beauty may fall (;)

through sweetkissed-rain

above sad whispers

this crush , (tells me she

is out of music)

sincerely time after a flood

could be delicious (but) this

ache always suited you

they hello me this shadow

and say; there was only above

may music

      (sweet

monster)   shine easy beneath my seat

cool beauty or beat poetry?

rimshot

I write poetry with punch lines
so you know they're over.
so maybe someone will get it
so the message is clear
so there's no doubt
and maybe the nugget of truth, of me,
hidden in there will be revealed.

but probably not.

there's a brilliant poet I knew:
he paints Mona Lisa's and the Sistine Chapel
before breakfast in words so light and transparent
the sky rains stained glass.

when he reads, hardly anyone applauds
until he's putting away the paper and moving on –
and they all ask him: "what did it mean?"

no one asks me that because
I write poetry with punch lines
so they laugh and they are done with it –
the applause come and I
still move on.

legal graffiti

my first apartment was like a refrigerator –
stark white institutional interior
units that all looked the same
with identical appliances and carpets
and glaring white walls which
we covered up with posters, held
with thumbtacks
at the corners

one night after drinking, I turned all the posters around
the colors and pictures and images were all gone
and the white backs matched the
white walls
and I wrote poetry on the backs of posters
all night drinking good beer
using a black magic marker –
down the hall, the living room, the bedrooms
words were everywhere
and all the places I looked
contained fragments of language
staring back at me

we left it that way for awhile
and people would stop by and find
us drinking beer and discussing different
lines: what it meant and didn't mean –
they must have thought we were mad

which we were

paying all that money for an apartment

with institutional walls

and a family of 12 living below us

children playing in the parking lot puddles

but we were happy, young, and drunk a lot of the time

eventually, we turned the posters around

and brought color back to the room

but those days when the walls breathed poetry

were beautiful and colorful

as any day since.

11.18.98

a Polaroid of us (is my prized possession) :
standing in the middle of Times Square freezing
amidst a million sparkling examples of Edison's pride & joy
illuminated by streetlamps and high on the scent of neon,
we're alone in a crowd surrounded by a concrete picket fence.
staring at the perpetual motion of friday night
following the scent of Marlboro's and your perfume
and i don't know why but dammit   you're an angel.
your blue eyes are blasphemy
cast in a face somewhere between Marilyn Monroe and silk...
      soft and unattainable.
i feel like you're flying away on a cloud of taxi exhaust
but i want to cut the steam of your breath
from the night
to put in my pocket.

falling on the grenade

she smokes too much
but I like to watch her slender fingers
hold the wrapper
flick the ash
holding it delicate as a promise.
fingertips, arms draped off the chair
and back to lips
lips that have whispered my name
precursor to the perfect 10 smile
lips that hold all the answers
to this mudball existence.

"hold this" she says
leaving me shivering
while she goes inside.

staring at night's playground,
imagining I see Orion's bellybutton
and Armstrong's flag on the moon:
absently puffing
on her cigarette
with a few coughs –
stargazing the darkness into a story
waiting for Laika's howl
and contemplating

the Little Bang.

finish it off, snub on the railing
guzzle more beer watching
a cumulus cloud collide
with my last gray puff of cancer –
covering stars I swore
looked like a police car two seconds ago.

she returns for the smoke
before she can ask:
"bad for you, so I smoked it."
surprise followed by confusion
as I stand on the bottom step –
then her smile
as she reaches for a fresh pack.
"you know," I say while she lights another,
"they always give medals for that
in the movies."

an open letter to Charles Simic

you don't remember me,
but years ago i walked down
that short hallway to your office
along the dull brown tile to
your door. nervous, i left a small
book of poems under your office door.
you were the world-renowned poet
just down the hall from my
introductory English professor -
i figured what the hell?
so I slid my best under the door
with a note asking for your
opinion, if you had the time.

no answer – not ever.
at first I was pissed off
you never got in touch –
righteous anger at the injustice
and i asked myself
what the hell does he know?
i was young and stupid, but
in some ways, i was right.

reading your poetry last night
i realized again how

subjective this beast
called Poetry really is.
good work by the way.

this world of words and
fractured sentences and
dangling ideas breeds equality.
with no way to pin this down
no chance at hemming it in
poetry grows wild on the streets
and in the libraries and down
at the local pub.
it may be try that
maybe only on my best and your worst days
we would be mentioned in the same
half-sentence,
but we're all equal out here Charles –
just something to think about.

therapy

Working at this
this right here
occupies my time
just fine.   You might say
                              this is mundane
                              or trite or
                              bland.

But this is my therapy –
this is why there's
no padded room with my name
on it. why i don't
ride a couch along
with the rest of
Prozac Nation.   On a high wire,
                              these words
                              are my Balance
                              and Luck.

Go ahead and laugh,
but this poem
just saved me
$150/hr.

suicide every morning

on the quiet city streets
still damp with night's silky residue
clinging to the sidewalks,
only the strongest and most desperate
awake as morning rounds the corner
too tight, leveling a crowd of garbage cans
sending rats and refuse hurtling
forward into the 8 am rush hour
traffic, full of morbid suits
rushing through the minutes.
shards of glass, mean-spirited drunks,
the meek and poor
are all swept away making room
for today's episode of blank-on-blank violence.

stained in between the cracks, hustlers
are the dull blade of humanity –
no longer a keen edge capable of
the quick slice that cleaves,
but instead hack and tear away
at the day's sinewy muscle
bringing slow death to
all around them.

drunks stumble over the bums
stumble over the dead stumble
over the policeman with his .45 caliber smile.

cats stalk the bird, aware of the game
but hungry and bored none the less.
like the rest of us.
like teenage vigilantes with nothing better
on their minds and volcanic hatred
in their hearts waiting for a shift.
like love with no peace and
harmony with no company
this kaleidoscope churns another day
forth without looking back.

wise man of the traffic jam

blank stares surround me, stuck in traffic at 5 pm
whirlwinds of red brake lights buzz through the exhaust
as radioactive hornets
wishing i smoked just for something to do,
my Zippo securely buried in my pocket
begging as my temper does for some reason to ignite
because these concrete paths are perfect for walking
which is what i want – light a cigarette and walk away
down these slim automobile alleyways
to parts unknown in our modern times,
traversing the smooth terrain between commuters
cigarette on lip, smoke filling lungs, sky filling eyes.
to hell with cancer:
we'll all die soon enough if the corporations have their way,
besides what's one pack gonna hurt?
that one perfect moment
of freedom is all i ask.

sitting two or three feet above the car roofs
in this mean-spirited diesel,
high above the lovers, the workers, and sinners
high above but not high enough,
it's just a matter or torque and horsepower to move
these others aside and push the diesel forward through,
but I enjoy this perch amongst the sheet metal,
high on my mountain like the wise man of the traffic jam.

Click-click
Click-click
snapping the Zippo lid
Open-shut
Open-shut

minutes pass seconds in the breakdown lane, wishing
there was a chrome-plated cigarette here to match my lighter
to match the dragrace sunset of winter through the smog.
the car in front inches forward more and more
an ant nudging its way along toward home
and i smile
because there's nowhere for me to go and I know
one inch doesn't buy much these days.
the diesel remains still and i return to daydreams of
unfiltered Camels and iron lungs.

looking at the sky, you'd never guess it was Monday
silky sulky purpleblue monster sucking up the
remaining shards of sunset and soon it will all be gone –
repackaged and rebranded as "evening" is commercials are
to be believed. nowhere to go
but places to be, just as these ants – somewhere to park
my mortal coil. they believe in places like somewhere and
i don't blame them – back home to a wife, husband, child, dog, etc.
my bed awaits nothing, empty as my pocket
refrigerator full of ketchup and two cans of beer
but it's a place to be.
which is why i suppose myself the wise man of the traffic jam:

not superiority – i just figured it out a little sooner than them.
we all learn sooner or later.

take this one for instance, fuming on a cell phone.
bellowing and steaming and fussing at some unseen ant
just that much further down the food chain than him.
just that much closer to the ground,
just that much closer to destitute. and he's...
wait... what's that? is it?

there's a wonderful pop to a truck door when it opens that first
inch and I savor the first gust of night mixed with diesel fumes,
swing the door wide and descend from the mountain
finding myself among the ants on the blacktop.

move around to the driver's side of a standard issue sedan
tap tap tap   on the ant's window
and like a goldfish he turns with open eyes and mouth
imagining that the entire world didn't see him there
inside his little bowl
the window shatters in a silence of mufflers and V6 engines
letting in the fumes, noise, and darkness
into his precious sanctuary

reaching past the shocked glare
past the jagged fierce teeth of glass
past the dull air and talk radio that fills his world
i retrieve a half pack of Camels.
throwing five dollars into his lap, i calmly turn and walk away
between the cars, guardrails, and highway signs

click open the Zippo, watch the flame leap into life,
then snap it closed along with the first drag.
behind me, more doors open and protests from the ants
compete with the idling engines.
walking away from my mountain, i decide to
take the long way home tonight.

turbulence

there's a vague mistrust of sleep
my legs ache with misuse
and tremble at rest
i should be running
that's what they tell me
i should be running
they spasm and quiver.
i'm at war with myself
and haven't chosen a side,
but i don't trust sleep...
not completely
and i don't really believe
in any of this.
this house, bed, floors,
money, cars, jobs, streetlamps...
imagining a giant wakeup call
eyes snap open
and all the world
will be vaguely familiar
and unrecognizable.

then,
i won't trust that
either.

suck honey from fuchsia

the hour is midnight and unimportant
unable to sleep,
i contemplate it all and try to imagine
some glimpse of what it
must be like to be God.
sleepless - watchful - patient
as i feel now when minutes
melt and trickle through my fingers.
dreaming angels and their mantra:
suck honey from fuchsia
forgot to leash my imagination today
now it's torn up my mind
and damn, all the dreams are shredded.
my trans-continental rift is adrift
and Pan the goat boy has the
next move in checkers. what?
it's all quite insane in the daylight
i know
but here in the nether-regions
of the morning , i can feel it
all gently pass like a crisp breeze
as we **suck honey from fuchsia**
and laugh over the endsum of this life.
the gentle ebb and flow of the
whole damn thing has me captivated with

desire – i feel sinful and holy as Satan

must have felt, seconds before being cast down...

i feel the day slipping in between the cracks

in night, the good filtering into the bad (or

the evil dipping its toe into the purity of

a sleeping woman's dream). the sensation

is a heated virginal tide that rises

as we **suck honey from fuchsia** and glide with

the waves that splash over us, threatening to

drown us all. black cats n ladders n the softness

of a smile at the breaking of day, jumbled

into a tumultuous garbage disposal of pop culture

and hell, maybe this could be the next hit power ballad

with the way the world has turned. no longer sure

of where when is or how long it'll be before

this moment has deserted me, i **suck honey from fuchsia**

and pray to some unforeseen complications that

this world will not melt away until i've had my

last few words read.

voices on the platform

waiting at the station – quarter to six
because the trains are late
again.
"maybe someone jumped on the tracks....
again" an educated woman offers.
"or got pushed" another voice comes "these
things happen all the damn time when i'm in a hurry..."
behind two stockbrokers in Wall Street Journal trench coats
of luxury, a man snickers
"don't anyone just hang themselves anymore?"

meanwhile, she is waiting
smoking a cigarette somewhere
with the truth glistening in crystal
eyes – maybe laughing
not wondering where i am.
waiting at the station i'll say
when i see her;
wanting to kiss her and hold my bundle of dreams
tightly in my weak arms
but i'll quietly sit
and ask   "how was your day?"

solitaire

thumb and forefinger
gentle scrubbing of lamination
nine of clubs passing slickly
over the 2 of diamonds
so far from shuffling
moving with purpose and a method
foreign to everyone else
in the room.

"there's many ways to play
solitaire"
she used to say

front to back
around to the side
and back to front

10 of spades
six of diamonds
ace of hearts
queen of diamonds

slipping around uncomfortably
but sure
just when it seemed over

to begin

again

"there's many ways to play

solitaire"

she used to say

permutations of numbers and

the house of royalty –

subjects

we avoided

numbering in the thousands

fifty-two ways

to lose

yourself

"there's many ways to play

solitaire"

she used to say

sucker punch

the message came through the line on a Tuesday
that she felt "violated"
by a poem i'd written and published
for "anyone to see".

the sun was shining and i was getting ready
for another day waiting on the ungrateful and cheap
but I thought fine – at least it touched someone.

in truth, there wasn't much truth to go around
except for this: she wanted me to leave
and a i left – belongings packed into boxes,
keys on the table.

after five years the dismissal came under cover of night
sitting in bed on a Sunday and it came like a sucker
punch out of nowhere – it kept on coming and coming
again and again for months and a year afterwards.

now, she's moved on and i've moved in
to another empty space that i'll dutifully keep warm
until someone else comes to take my place, trying to
decide if breathing is still a good way to pass the time.

but she felt "violated" and in the end, there are
things that we never stop paying for – and even though
no harm was ever intended, a response is necessary

one without ambiguity.

so just to be clear, this poem is about you
and it doesn't mean any harm –
it's the only way I can keep living each day
and I'm sorry if that offends you,
but that's the way life goes.

peace in our time

much like the Gulf of Tonkin, the details don't matter
not anymore
only shadows remain from what had become
and inevitable spark, but
my Vietnam was the day i knew her love was gone.

the end was another glorified beginning,
digging into trenches, digging into the mud
her eyes became tracers in the night air,
her hair barbed wire cutting deep
my heart a grenade with the pin pulled.

my Vietnam continued for months and years:
incapable of securing victory, refusing to acknowledge defeat
over-supplied and under-motivated
the landscape dotted with smoking craters
and the smell of wet rot.

the details don't matter much
when she kissed that other man
when love left us both
who fired first
no peace, no surrender was our motto.

digging in for the last stand, knowing the protests
waiting, surrounded by the collateral damage,
finally retreating to the rooftop when

through smoke, i saw clearly and moved
for the door.

life packed into cardboard boxes – no spoils of war
or moral victory – only casualties.
and when the helicopters lifted off, i knew
that this "police action"
was more out of duty
than Love.

sea wall

with the sun directly overhead,
drove to the ocean
to taste salty air and clear
the cobwebs from my memory.
sitting on the sea wall
I am a freak
because I'm holding a book of poetry
with fingertips numb from
the early spring breeze
alone.

the parents walk by with unwanted
and wanted children,
wondering if I'm some sort
of pervert or sex fiend. the old
walk by wondering if I'll rob them.
the others just walk by
because they are "good people"
with husbands, wives, mortgages,
solid jobs, bright futures, and stability
at home.

the poems taste of salt and spring
and I forgive each and every
other freak as they pass -
(even as I question: am I a sex fiend?
am I strange?)

they don't know any better.

surveying the driftwood and sea glass
between poems
dropping memories into the surf
like paper lanterns
letting the tide carry them
out to sea where they'll
burn brightly as good little pyromaniacs dream

they'll become message bottles for someone
else to find and love.

a love letter to Mrs. Castro

My dear – My goddess.
this star shines on you
running my fingers through
your raven hair as I ran though a
field of beauty as a child
touching your cocoa thighs
kissing your smooth neck
scented of rose and juniper
whispering your name
to the sugarcane
and foolish moon.

you move like a weary shadow
over my bed in the darkness
a jubilant ghost
glad to be alive.
your laugh, so familiar –
won't you laugh
with me tonight?
playful muse, you dance on the shore
reveling in this holiest of communions.
My dear – My goddess.
if only Stalin knew,
he'd be green with envy.

sometimes, a wonder of wild roses

dawns over her headboard
Sunday
and the trains have
stopped
the cars
have stopped
and stopped, even have
the people

when sun careens through
the windowpane,
lighting her candle-eyes
which looking
at me
seem
to cry a million years
laugh
a thousand tears
and dance me
into the next room
before
"good morning"
ever is
born.

this blissful
eternity of cotton, sunlight

and skin –

communion of the

secret order

of rose petals

and kiss

ours to savor.

delight in your eyes

who wrote the rules ?
of when   howmuchandwhere I cancannot
kiss your lips and   hold true
your body
neatly next to mine and whisper
in your ear.   what if ...
we met in the supermarket on aisle 3
between rice and pasta
and i kissed your neck ...!
 (right thenandthere and you turned
  slapped my face   and frantically
  dashed to the soup section)
would you think it strange ?
what about in the bread aisle ...?

no long goodbyes

Standing in the desert town,
fire escapes cling and grow
relentlessly against the brick –
thick as ivy on cathedral walls
built by righteous sinners.
Taking one last look around
before the train leaves

before I'm riding across fields and rivers
feeling the bump and clatter of
steel tracks meeting steel wheel;
held by faith and a notion
passing through a country I barely
know.

Looking around one last time:
shutters open and shut
alternately welcoming and shunning
me from the sidewalk
where hip and desperate people
wait to slowly die;
fading daily a little bit more
into gray paste
until they fill another cement crack
with another cement dream.

And leave their families behind
to wonder: "what happened to _____?"

August rains

I've been sitting in this house for months
with these animals, my books,
and nothing to do but look
outside at the Good People of the world

they go to work
come home to their families
fight, make love, fight some more
and go back to work

the rain has been falling
for a couple days   and
the streets are quieter right now

no one can understand it, but I love
rain as I'd love god or a beautiful woman –

it adds this wonderful shade of
transparent gray
washing away the dust

I glance outside and see one of the cats
sitting underneath my car
and he's looking out into the rain – and
I marvel at how this animal
that's taken for granted lives his own little
life inside that fur

and he's staring at the rain like me
wondering what to do next
(just like me)

it's coming down hard in heavy drops
that smack onto the pavement
and create the most beautiful
racket I've heard since someone played
John Coltrane's "A Love Supreme" backwards
at the same time as a Beethoven sonata

looking back, the cat has drifted off to sleep
under the car, despite the thunder
vibrating through the trees and between
the houses

I love the rain as I love old
girlfriends -

except the rain always comes back

greetings from wherever you are:

the weather has turned here
and a frozen wind embraces
the unlucky few to be caught outside.

nights full of ice and dreaming heartache
      (and of course your name came up)
dreaming a thousands miles covered in highway
oceans of asphalt separating us

and it isn't enough for me.

the nights are getting longer here
and all the friendly faces
belong to ghosts that barely know
my name as they shuffle through
on their way along the roads
to God only knows where.

before the winter, we had some times
didn't we? but that was years ago
now but even before the first frost
your heart was 3 feet deep with snow.

to my friend, my secret liar –
i hope life treats you well.

the sweet science

it gets so I get drunk
bare-knuckled and drunk
Bukowski drunk
Morrison drunk
Edgar Allen Poe drunk
Hemingway drunk
to go 12 rounds with the demon
and I hit that motherfucker
right in the teeth
hard

left, left, then right
combinations changing, always moving
always moving and keeping just
out of reach – left, right, left, left, right
always moving

keep my hands up
the hits come in overhand anyways
rights, uppercuts, jabs, and all
manner of twisted wild strikes

so i wind up good from
the bottom of my shoes and
the bottom of this bottle

and land this roundhouse blow
before retreating at the bell
back to my corner, surveying the damage.

across the ring, the demon spits
with glazed eyes – damaged and staggered
but unwilling to accept defeat.
not yet.

it gets so after 12 rounds all i want to do
is hit and keep hitting until
the whole world is a softened bag
easy to handle
easy to hit

eventually, the judges call in their decision
for this night and when slumber
can't be shrugged off any longer
i retire to dream it all away
before waking to the warm sunlight
screaming through the window
like a million death blossoms
floating on the breeze
pouring through milk white blinds

and i am convinced
that one more day
really isn't all that bad.

i never wear a watch

i measure time by women

some people use watches
or sundials
or calendars

but i've found that
it's easiest to remember
when this one left
that one came

the night she
stood naked in the window
laughing on cheap wine
while the moonlight streamed
in, coating her in a thick
layer of shimmering glow

september 6th 1999

see, now wasn't that
easy?

temperamental animals

this cat and i have been in the same foxhole
now for years, and he's as good a companion
that anyone could ask for:

the ever present night watchman
staring out into night as black as
his own fur

quiet, decently mannered, perhaps
a little on the temperamental side –
but otherwise a good sort.

unwilling to purr for just anything
or anyone, there's a delicate ceremony

his affection isn't given freely,
it has to be worked for.

the women come and go
most times with the same lines:
"it isn't you, it's me –
this just won't work..."

sure honey, whatever you say

the cat stares through his calm
yellow eyes,

waiting

asking

"another one gone, eh?"

a sigh and then nod –

another one gone. perhaps

i'm too temperamental

needing more upkeep than usual

not willing to purr for just anything

or anybody.

slowly he drifts off to sleep, leaving

me to my ways and madness

wondering when the next one

will come through the door.

an odd pair, we're both of a

good sort i think –

even though we don't give

our love all at once

and need more attention than average.

miller time

there's a lot of good things in this world

but sometimes... I'm not one of them.

there should be some reason
why a good, simple line of poetry
would strike through all the muck
and bullshit and red tape,
heartbreak, sadness, depression,
throbbing hemorrhoids, gut aches,
painful nightmares, vivid daydreams,
and the gaunt reality of another
day in a land where the air
is supposed to be free
but clouds over with disappointment
packed in with
another layer of soot
and toxic radioactive fallout
spewed from the asshole
of another elected official
on the dole.

what, did I stutter or
are you surprised? you shouldn't
be, but then again
nobody pays attention
anymore.

the job doesn't pay.

there's a lot of
good things
in this world,
I'm not one of them tonight.

because sitting here inside my warm
cocoon of a home, staring
at candles melting down the seconds,
I'm wondering about bills, money, filthy
whoring commerce, and what's
for dinner tomorrow (beef you stupid
motherfucker beef, it's what's for dinner
now get on with it... okay...) and pondering
just how in the world
heaven or hell could god – god no less –
be thinking about this
soul sitting here tapping out
a few words per minute
over a half-finished beer. but it's
true enough I guess because
otherwise, there's
no good explanation for being here
or there or anywhere
else.

there's
a lot of good things in this world.

this next beer will hopefully be
one
of
them.

one minute short of forever

I was laying on my bed
listening to the rain pour down outside
from deep inside the Virginia
sky
the world seemed like a calm place
for a moment

laying there with no money
no dreams
and no woman
and after drinking a pot of coffee
the room looked hateful
and full of spite

and I laughed

because it all seemed so poetical
that the entire
swirling mess of insanity
was in the room with me
one minute short of forever
and waiting for more

she is gone and she left
and she is still there but different
she is waiting for me later
and she won't wait any longer

the whole mass of confusion

makes for one long joke

and the punchline always seems to be me

making plans to work another

night and let life have its course

one more time

and maybe the planet

won't fall of its axis if

the rain doesn't wash us

away

first.

the luckiest man alive

he's a gray-haired man with a bulldog stance
well-worn face of scars
and a limp –
but he'd tell anyone who'd listen
that he was the luckiest man alive.

standing in the coffeehouse
looking for any soul to talk at
or a fight (whichever came first –
he didn't particularly care).

"I been dead five times," he began
"and I'm still standing here – I ain't
afraid of nobody living or dead."
and I believed him because after all,
there he stood, just as alive as any
of us in that line, maybe moreso.

he had this way of dancing or
sliding towards me and then away
like a boxer weaving around the ring
while he spun one story after another.

his wife worked behind the counter
and helped him with the stories.
neither of them had any front teeth
but she was proud of him:

the lack of fear and his stories.

"I'm the luckiest man alive," he'd say
while she laughed and poured
more coffee into my cup.

maybe he's right.

choices

you can keep your money and fame
popping flashbulb walks down red carpets
and the women –
fuck it, keep it all because I have it figured out
after years of stumbling over my words
and begging for the next beautiful woman
to set me free and save my soul –

choice

power is temporary and highs are expensive
keep your heroin(e) and keep
your luxury condo, your limousines, models
expensive champagne and gold chains

it all comes down to choice

those who choose hold the power
and the world

and the bitch is:
we all have the power
but
some don't know it

I didn't

sitting curled in a corner with my fears
as a blanket, I prayed for her to keep me safe
and dreamt her name until
it was tattooed on my brain
in brilliant colors of red and purple –
until the day she chose for me to leave

now I know that this
forced independence has merit
and that I've been living the life of a Fool
for years

this life of semi-squalor, living paycheck to paycheck
and wondering quietly to myself
if I'll have the rent money by the first
or enough to procure a six-pack or
if I can afford to cut my hair or if I'll just shave my head
but these are all choices
and I treasure them
even the difficult ones

choosing to work for less than I'm worth
affording time to get
this all down onto paper
get it all down, get it all down
so that maybe someone will feel it
maybe someone will
love this and hold it
maybe they'll choose
me.

get in the car

waking in the middle of the night
situation unknown
crawling for the protection
of the nearest corner,
back in,
and breath.

from the garage, from
deep in the center
of whoever I am today
in a voice only heard
by me the word repeats:
run.

the cry of a schizophrenic
monk, chanting through
clenched dirty teeth
run run run run run run run
never to stop – keep
moving. get in the car
, turn the radio loud
over the screaming protest
of the engine
and never let off the gas.

make the scenery blur
in the windows – keep

the earth rotating, keep it
grinding on that axis, spinning
until that lonely spark
ignites and we all
go up in a puff
of filthy smoke.

one word
becomes more of the same
the chant continues
and the earth
creaks on its rusty poles
somebody needs to grease
the wheel – someone
needs to gag
the monk, someone needs
to stop us all
before it's too late…

here we go now.

we're burning now – burning
and running with
the pedal to the floor
and no brakes or breaks with
nothing but smoke filling
the windshield.

burning and burning
catching more flames,

holding them in our hands
running with
the flames
speeding across the
countryside , sparks
flying everywhere
set the world ablaze

until the
quiet

deafens us all

and only the echoes of the chant remain.
only the eavesdroppers
survive. "Just get in the car"
I say
"We can still make the
coast
by dawn"

gurrrlllz

the word rolled off his tongue
just as I imagined
Dean Moriarty woulda said it :

"gurrrlllz..."

not a question or answer ;
no statements here ,
just a signed confession of infatuation
full of longing and cruelty.

"gurrrlllz..."

they were beautiful that day,
swarming by the dozen
past the window
in short dresses and shorts
two sizes too small :
sun on their smiles
laughter in their eyes,
everything in front of them
before growing old and weathered :
beaten down by men and
themselves

"gurrrlllz..."

they moved past in great waves
of perfume and perfectly crafted
hair while we sipped beer and hid
ourselves from the daylight.

"gurrrlllz..."

none meant for us, but
it passed the time
on a Sunday afternoon.

the world dies each sunday at 7:38 pm

No calls returned
the dial tone is the most unfriendly knife in the drawer
cutting and cutting and cutting out the night
and the rain
and the rain
keeps falling until it reaches the neck
then the eyes
before too long, the evening disappears
underneath the torrential showers of early Spring
the gravy on this starlit night
a series of clouds rolling through to the North
and the South and the West (with the East
gracefully abstaining) according to the
well-groomed meteorologist on channel 41

the world takes its sleeping pill early
on Sunday and snores through another vengeful night
while I prowl through the hours
and the minutes and the moments
so dusty and neglected
until the morning shines through windows
like a jailbreak spotlight
under God's microscope
under the cloud's eye patch

dismembered days do the tango
a dangerous dance of disenchantment

over my eyelids

trying to sleep

trying to sleep

trying to sleep

until it has the better of me

the worst of me

everything between

and the fireplace moans for another victim

another wooden sacrifice

to fuel the night – just a little longer

it begs

just a little

longer.

Ben Carr at the Alamo

half-past midnight:
and I'm talking for my life.

one foot in this moment
the other in a dream
shifting back and forth
I can almost dance
through this night
without losing my pride

a sinner, I know
(but aren't we all)
no answers from the bartender,
imagining at this last stand
the only thing left
is dance –
maybe her vision is clear
seeing through charlatan words
and find something
(anything)
she likes

dancing for my supper
and my life
just like Ben Carr
somewhere tonight

love and madness

have their price

but at least the ride is fun.

the job description

I think our world is fucked.

There
I've said it -
you don't have to.

You can continue
on about your day
with family, friends,
job, mortgage,
and enemies
without having to come
right out and
say it.

The words won't come
in your sleep, and you
won't need to wear
the edge from the night
with beer after beer –
your nightmares
can be put to bed
now.

You aren't sitting at
this keyboard
waiting for the whole

thing to blow in
our faces.

I think our world is fucked.

There
I've said it -
you don't have to.

You're welcome.

Mr. Ani DiFranco

then there was the night
I was going to marry Ani DiFranco.

the bottle of Jack Daniels was
a lighthouse on the nightstand
and we'd been alternately listening
to Lester Young since 10 am
that morning.

staring across the pillowcase
at her wry smile
I'd say "why not?"
and she'd laugh
into the crisp white linen
twisting the sheets around her
and I'd almost yank the
end with all my might just
to watch her gyroscope spin
through the room.

we'd be halfway across the state
and find this ancient Shaker meeting house
piloted by an old hippie preacher
by the side of the road
and we'd say "I do"
sipping wine to the left
of the small Jerry Garcia shrine

by the offering plates.
maybe the wedding could be
bigger –
except that I'd always
wonder for my life
if it was my you smiled at
walking down the aisle
of a bridesmaid.

collect

calling all frequencies, all
ships at sea
and lost mothers with glass-eye souls
this is
midnight calling overdue
as we dance through the gates
and laugh into the sun

obscene ideas become mild
and meek overthrow the
wicked
this is midnight calling overdue
dawn will be upon us
soon
and before darkness parts
ways with moon

the intergalactic busy signal
will bounce through
the coffins of the living
and laugh into the cathedral
shouting
this is midnight calling collect
with the circus trainer's daughter
in my Chevrolet
tonight

and we're not coming
back to this place
anymore
with these people
and these dreams
have been
deemed
inadmissible as evidence

your honor,
I swear it was
the demon
with blue eyes.

all the sweet women are gone

as lilacs in September

sitting among the beer bottles

seaweed and rock –

gulls cackle over the Atlantic

at obscene jokes

whispered between sun and sea.

Alone with the wind

the women are gone :

sweet and sour

(gone alike)

tide inching forward

waiting

until I go

as well.

high noon

okay Lord, it's just You and me
now don't try and stop me
because just before noon we're heading out there
and it's gonna go down like this

You head north and I'll go south
at the appropriate, civilized interval
we'll turn and face
to wait for Time to dictate the starting point

after all, we have to be rational about this, right?

now don't try an' talk me outta this Lord
because we all know this has been comin'
for quite some time now don't we?

You just stand down there yonder at the end of
Main Street and look me in the eye –
I'll do my best to look You right there too partner, and
we'll just see how this thing ends up.

but in the meantime, let's pour one more whiskey
and forget about that clock hangin' crooked
over on that wall now, okay? be civilized about
this here thing if You get what I'm saying.

idiot savant

they're always encouraging
me – egging
me on – promoting my
addiction and glorifying
the disease

that's what it can be

a blessing
a disease
a curse
a catharsis

i don't sit and try to write poems
because they come to me

good, bad, indifferent

which some think is
brilliance
and others find to
be a disquieting birth
defect

most days, it's fun
to play with words, make them
do things

they're not supposed
to do –

but at night when
the beer has run out,
the light bill is late,
there's not enough oil
left to turn on the heat
and all I can do is pour
out line
after line
after line

shivering and drunk
like a hound trying to tree
his prey

it isn't that glamorous.

lifespan

The evening news said that
citizens of the United States
were living longer than ever now.

More time to work, more time to
waste, more time to spend money
on unnecessary shit, more time
to drink away pain, more time to
ignore the poor, more time to
extol the rich, more time to whither
in old age, and more time
to ponder
if a life sentence
is that much
better than
the electric
chair.

Living longer than ever now
with more vices and amusement
than anyone knows what to do
with and fewer reasons to
Fill that excess life
with something beautiful
rather than fear and hate.

Congratulations America.

resting in the hours and minutes

the cat rests on the sunny carpet
in the warm confines of his fur –

we've come to Maine this
November for the same woman
a raven-haired beauty
with a contagious laugh
and soft lips.

he arrived before me
and has adopted his new home
with ease – moreso than any other
we've been to together.

today he rests on the living room
floor in grateful worship of the
sun and shelter from the wind
tossing leaves outside.

every few moments, he raises
his head and cracks those
Halloween eyes with the
recognition of
oh, it's you again
and then is off to sleep again.

we make a good team:

he pretends to sleep
and I pretend to write.

black and white newsreel

thousands of stillframes caught in time, held in place
sprockets and borders tying them together in long
celluloid chains: dogs, fire hoses, and teargas
with "America the Beautiful" as sonic backdrop

because inner city blues do make me wanna holler
Marvin – make a man wanna holler "I don't wish
I were black, but there's a lotta times I wish I
wasn't white"

Zappa had it right. he had a point. he had a bead on
it – because the "land of the free" has a lot of fine print
to read at the bottom of the page. it's free if you aren't
a woman who wanted to vote. free if you aren't a
black man who wants to live. free if you have the right
skin and the right religion and the right attitude. free
if you aren't all that picky about being free.

when I think that 40 years ago a man couldn't get
a sandwich or a cup of coffee without risking his neck
because it was the wrong color, I wanna holler. every time
a newsman says "terrorist action" I think about implicit
support of Jim Crow, Rosa Parks, Malcolm X and
Dr. Martin Luther King, Jr.
cold and dead
Billy Holiday's "Strange Fruit", nameless graves,
lynchings, rapes, murders, dehumanizations.

and now we're the measure of freedom, some forty or
fifty years on – a beacon to the rest of the world some
three or four generations past standing in the schoolhouse
door – judge, jury, and executioner for the rights of many.

doesn't anyone else see the red of the flag not just as blood
shed in the name of freedom and liberty,
but also in the prejudice?
in the name of protest? in the name of difference?
in the name of the father, son, and holy ghost as well?
in the name of Crispus Attucks –
a man killed in revolution that didn't revolve around him?
every time I hear someone say "kill 'em all and let God
sort 'em out" or "it's us or them" I wanna holler
because we're not that far from
1939 Germany in more than one way.

the blue of the flag isn't just for the sea to shining sea promise
of the country, but the dirty grabbing hands that ripped
away the land in between through the years. it's
the frozen fingers
of citizens living on street corners and ignored, forgotten, and
left to die. it's the sky blue promise unfulfilled to the working
class as they dig their own graves each day a
little
bit
deeper.

is it too late for America to turn and look in the mirror?
too late to notice we're not all that much different

all that much better
all that much worse
than anyone anywhere?
too late to notice that once you've looked down your
nose at the world, it's only a short step from being
stepped on?

can I get a witness?

that the white in the stars is the skin of a slave master?
the tooth knocked out in Chicago outside the convention?
the eyes of a young man being thrown into a detention
camp in Southern California, 1943?

wasn't that long ago was it?

can someone – anyone – out there notice all this,
give me a witness, and tell me how on earth
we can cast that first stone?

I tell ya... makes me wanna holler.

the ultimate reward

under the glow of a 60-watt bulb, she asked another question:
what's it like to write a poem?

it was after a few beers and I'm sure the answer
was nothing short of charming and completely misleading

but here's an answer
just a few years too late.

it's like dragging all your skeletons
out of the closet at once for Spring Cleaning –
like holding a garage sale of the soul

all of your dirty laundry (including the
underwear with stains) on display for the world to see

it's showing your soft underbelly and waiting
to see if anyone will come in for the kill

I have a theory that all poets secretly wait and pray for Death:

only then will anyone read our words
and think them legendary, epic, or even worthwhile

maybe it's all the fault of agents or bad love
or not being able to feel love at all

but that's what it's like – a compulsive
debilitating disease that at once tears you down
and gives you peace.

more addictive than heroin or applause
lethal as the air we breath
and necessary as every second
melts off the great clockworks.

because someone should;

Beauty drops in,
her coffee-brown hair
a tango in Havana
a breeze in Paris
a gondola in Venice.

standing in a cage of sunshine
her sparking eyes,
secret smile all their own:

with breath held
i wish a dozen
Valentine-red roses
to her door.

Love, in the Nuclear Age

my lust is radioactive
glowing as chrome
from a mint green and orange
1950's dinette set

this dream is a hole in time –
burrowing back beyond Ike
in the White House, when
rock n' roll was a gleam in the
blind eye of a broke Delta
bluesman.

back before
the most boring of decades
when pipe smoking husbands
chuckled reading the evening news
while apron wearing wives
baked and cleaned their
lives away.

our love is at the sub-atomic,
born long before anyone
ever knew what
an "atom"
was.

i see it in your electron eyes,

burning in my protons –
when we get together,
it's Los Alamos all over
again.

Todo se aparta sin danar la hora

To one side, not bruising the hour
she stretches in the sunshine
corridor between
gasps of forever, before
the crime of morning is done.

To one side, not bruising the hour
pregnant clouds patrol the skies,
gray with worry and discontent –
wolves and children
companions in the mist.

To one side, not bruising the hour
Death shuffles through a crowded
railroad terminal, oblivious
to delays and lost luggage
but ever mindful of the clock.

To one side, not bruising the hour
we hold hands on the beach
when the moon chases the sun off his porch
embraced while the waves
held vigil this night and ever after.

To one side, not bruising the hour
mankind marches along to its
own dim outcome : kind and cruel,

bound for destruction
en masse suicide.

To one side, not bruising the hour
we cradle hope in this storm's eye
and kiss the swirling chaos away.
If Love can live here, maybe
time will grant a stay.

You're sleeping in the next room

and the rain is pouring down
and the clock is pushing through another lap
and the cat is watching over the moon
and the keyboard is breathing fire again –
just like the old days.

Except now I have a home and
have become respectable.
2 glasses of wine and yawned.
i don't go mad at 1 am anymore
with tears stinging my eyes
for forgotten reasons. The
mortgage was on time, the bills
are paid (and on time no less).

I've become domesticated
and you never met that other guy
filled with madness, desperation, and
fatalistic, suicide laughter. The one
who drank with servants and kings,
raging into the darkness until
the night spat him back out.

In a way, I'm sad because that guy
could be a lot of fun given the
proper circumstances (not
usually, but sometimes). Mostly,

on nights like this when I wonder
what it's be like to still have that
guy around – I smile and wave
good-bye to the memories, click
off the light and slip away –

happy to be here half-crazy with
you sleeping in the next room
rather than fully crazy
anywhere else.

to my little cherry bomb --

standing inside the moment,
our first kiss hanging in the air between us
a hazy daydream awaiting an owner,
fearless and sure were two hearts
falling as the cascading embers
of a roman candle through the
night sky. a split-second in time
when the world, in danger
of ignition (given the proper
match strike), holds its breath
in anticipation of this...

one highly flammable kiss
between lovers-to-be.

tightly compressed in our
explosion of passion, the
fuse long gone in a puff of
smoke, the only difference
being creation over destruction –

because in an explosion
everything is up for grabs.

all of them there in a row

first, there was the one in high school
who wound up marrying my best friend
but could never return my affection because we
were too close. she drove me to poetry and suicidal tendencies.

then there was the one in college who was kind
and I turned away for a crazy whore.
she drove me to drink and nights of screaming.

of course, we can't forget the one with soft
blonde curls who had a taste for frat boys and
making me crawl. she drove me to better poetry and whiskey.

the one with deep brown eyes that kept her eyes
on the macho rich boys that treated her like shit
made me even better.

ah, and who could forget the one who decided
it was time to go in the middle of the night. she
drove me to another state altogether.

finally there was the one who thought salvation
could be bought in a self-help book.

now, I live with one who is kind, funny, and in
retrospect surpasses them all.
so where the hell was she all those years?

Todd Regoulinsky...

...was born and raised in New Hampshire, moved to Virginia, has sipped pints in Ireland, honeymooned in Canada, and someday hopes to visit Timbuktu.

...studied at the University of New Hampshire and has worked as a stockroom picker, waiter, website designer, printer, bartender, and delivery driver.

...has been published in *Freefall* and *Aegis* magazines and possibly more places if you're interested in making use of the future tense.

...currently lives in Maine with his wife and daughter where he finally realized that there's no figuring it all out, just getting it all out.

If such things interest you, he can be reached on his personal website located at toddregoulinsky.com 24/7.

www.ingramcontent.com/pod-product-compliance
Lightning Source LLC
Chambersburg PA
CBHW031554300426
44111CB00006BA/315